PORTLAND (Ore.)
The Delaplaine
2021 Long Weekend Guide

Andrew Delaplaine

GET 3 FREE NOVELS
Like political thrillers?
See next page to download 3 great page-turners—
FREE - no strings attached.

NO BUSINESS HAS PAID A SINGLE PENNY OR GIVEN *ANYTHING* TO BE INCLUDED IN THIS BOOK.

A list of the author's other travel guides, as well as his political thrillers and titles for children, can be found at the end of this book.

Senior Editors - *Renee & Sophie Delaplaine*
Senior Writer - **James Cubby**

Gramercy Park Press
New York – London – Paris
Copyright © by Gramercy Park Press - All rights reserved.

WANT 3 FREE THRILLERS?
Why, of course you do!
If you like these writers--
Vince Flynn, Brad Thor, Tom Clancy, James Patterson, David Baldacci, John Grisham, Brad Meltzer, Daniel Silva, Don DeLillo
If you like these TV series –
House of Cards, Scandal, West Wing, The Good Wife, Madam Secretary, Designated Survivor

> You'll love the **unputdownable** series about Jack Houston St. Clair, with political intrigue, romance, and loads of action and suspense.

Besides writing travel books, I've written political thrillers for many years that have delighted hundreds of thousands of readers. I want to introduce you to my work!
Send me an email and I'll send you a link where you can download the first 3 books in my bestselling series, absolutely FREE.

Mention **this book** when you email me.
andrewdelaplaine@mac.com

PORTLAND (Ore.)
The Delaplaine Long Weekend Guide

TABLE OF CONTENTS

Chapter 1 – WHY PORTLAND? – 5

Chapter 2 – GETTING ABOUT – 9

Chapter 3 – WHERE TO STAY – 12

Chapter 4 – WHERE TO EAT – 25

Chapter 5 – NIGHTLIFE – 60

Chapter 6 – WHAT TO SEE & DO – 68

Chapter 7 – SHOPPING & SERVICES – 79

INDEX – 89

Other Books by this Author – 94

Chapter 1
WHY PORTLAND

DID YOU FIND AN INTERESTING PLACE?
If you discover a place you think I should check out on my next visit, drop me a line, will you? I'll mention your name if I end up listing it.
andrewdelaplaine@mac.com

The first thing that strikes you visually when you get into Portland is how GREEN everything is. This has a lot to do with the climate: it's on the wet side in the winter (warm and dry in the summer), but it's a mild wet and so everything is green. (It's not nearly as wet as Seattle, but then nowhere is.) The city has innumerable parks and other open spaces that take full advantage of this lovely climate.

The town is green in another way, in a proactively eco-friendly way, and this concerned attitude toward the environment is evident top to bottom, from the mayor down to the guy collecting the trash three times a week. These people are concerned on a daily basis about the quality of the place where they live and everything in Portland is designed to project this reality. (As a visitor, this is apparent in the high quality of Portland's public transportation system.)

The city lies between Seattle and San Francisco, and is a kind of mix between those two larger and wildly distinctive cultural entities.

Portland is situated where two great rivers converge, the Willamette and the Columbia. About 50 miles to the east you can't miss Mount Hood rising majestically into the sky, the highest mountain in Oregon. (It's on virtually every postcard picturing Portland.) Also in the distance you can see the snow-capped pile that is mount Saint Helens, the famous volcano that in 1980 suffered a cataclysmic eruption that killed everything for miles around it.

The people of Portland who call this place home include the 2 million+ in the Metro area and the 600,000 in the city proper. Like its two neighbors, it's got a little of Seattle and a little of San Francisco: markedly liberal and quick to tell you so, lots of what we used to quaintly call "bohemians," lots of very smart people and lots of people who treasure the outdoors lifestyle.

One good reason to visit Portland all by itself is its outstanding collection of prized microbreweries. These people know their beer. When the people aren't drinking beer, they're most certainly drinking coffee! Curiously enough, in an era when the publishing industry worldwide is suffering losses to the digital world, Portland has become a center where the industry thrives. There are numerous interesting publications to be found in Portland, and I suppose all the people in the brewpubs and coffee shops are reading them.

But it's not all about the beer. It's also about the arts. Portland is home to thousands of accomplished artists working in every field and is considered one of the top 10 destinations among those who travel to enjoy the arts.

You have to check out the **Pearl District**. It's an area flooded by young people with a little more money than people have in other parts of town. It's trendy, with great boutiques and a good variety of restaurant and café choices. Some people think it's snobby, but I think they're just jealous.

There's a new section of Portland, the **Central Eastside Industrial District** (which itself is a part of the **Inner Southeast**). It has become sort of the Brooklyn to Portland's Manhattan. The unabashedly gritty industrial area has attracted a growing legion of plucky young entrepreneurs, shop owners and restaurateurs who continue to open new and edgy places. (I've listed several of them below.)

Central Eastside is just east of the Willamette River, and while it's not as touristy, you'll certainly benefit from going through the area. It's within walking distance to Downtown, and there's the **Portland Streetcar**, a new line that runs through this whole area and makes getting there from Downtown effortless: www.portlandstreetcar.org

Tourist Information
Portland Visitor Information & Services Center
701 SW Sixth Ave (at Morrison), 503-275-8355
www.travelportland.com

Chapter 2
GETTING ABOUT

From the Airport
It can cost $40 for a taxi from Portland International Airport (PDX), but because Portland has such an innovative (and integrated) transportation system, you can use it the minute you leave the airport. Hook into the **MAX Red Line** at the airport. It's conveniently located next to baggage claim. The half-hour ride to downtown costs a couple of dollars. Hold on to your ticket because it's good for unlimited transfers for up to 2 hours. Using that ticket, you can transfer to **Trimet** buses or **C-TRAN** buses.

In a Car
If you're in a rental car, remember there are no gas stations in the immediate vicinity of the airport so you won't be able to fill up your tank when you return it. (I found out the hard way.) Plan ahead. **Avoid Downtown** if you're driving. Just forget about it. It's congested. There's no parking to be had and it's just a general pain in the ass. Aggressive meter maids writing parking tickets (from 8 A.M. till 7 P.M.) like they're going out of style. Park the car and use public transit. (Hell, you can walk across the whole city in 20 minutes.)

Bicycles
A lot of the roads here are designed around bicyclists, not motorists. This is such a bike friendly city it's sometimes called ""Bicycle Capital." Major thoroughfares have bike lanes. Waterproof maps of the dozens of bike trails and bike lanes are available from Metro - www.oregonmetro.gov - for a small fee. Well worth it if you're a cyclist. Tired of cycling? Hop on a MAX line or any bus, bikes are welcome.

Public Transit
Buses, streetcars, light-rail trains are all operated by **Trimet** - www.trimet.org. If you're in Portland, get to know the system well. It's among the best in the country.

MAX is the light-rail system in which Portland has made a large investment. In addition to the 4 MAX lines, the4re are 2 **Streetcar** lines.

Chapter 3
WHERE TO STAY

DID YOU FIND AN INTERESTING PLACE?
If you discover a place you think I should check out on my next visit, drop me a line, will you? I'll mention your name if I end up listing it.
andrewdelaplaine@mac.com

THE ACE HOTEL
1022 SW Stark St., 503-228-2277
acehotel.com
Located in Portland's historic downtown in a 4-floor 1912 building is this trendy little boutique hotel. The rooms are so unpretentious they look like spiffed up

dorm rooms in some college. There are lots of different rooms "types," so look at 2 or 3 before deciding which one to stay in. Can't beat this place for price, location and lively youthful atmosphere.

FULTON HOUSE BED & BREAKFAST
7006 SW Virginia Ave, 503-892-5781
www.thefultonhouse.com
South Portland, one block west of Willamette Park. The Fulton House features a "Craftsman style" design. This late 19th century home features modern amenities: four spacious guest rooms (with private baths), cable flat screen TVs, DVD and CD players, free telephones and high speed Wi-Fi. Homemade breakfast served each morning in a formal dining room. (The main floor has a kitchen where your breakfast is prepared.) The living room is filled with hundreds of books and many antiques. Relax with a

glass of wine on the outdoor patio or soak in the luxurious hot tub, or simply sit by the Koi pond and listen to the peaceful waterfall. Free street parking in this quiet neighborhood is readily available.

THE HEATHMAN
1001 SW Broadway, Portland, 503-241-4100
www.heathmanhotel.com
Built in 1927, this upscale landmark hotel features 150 luxurious guest rooms and suites with Art Deco style interiors juxtaposed with modern art by the likes of Warhol, Hap Tivey and Henk Pender. Amenities include: flat-screen TVs, complimentary Wi-Fi, and a book lending library. Hotel facilities include: multiple dining options (they have a really good brunch on weekends), and fitness center. Conveniently located across the street from the Arlene Schnitzer Concert Hall.

HOSTELLING INTERNATIONAL PORTLAND-NORTHWEST,
479 NW 18th Ave. (at NW Glisan St.), 503-241-2783
www.nwportlandhostel.com
Not only is this place incredibly cheap, it's perfectly located so you can walk to everything in Portland's historic district. It's located in 2 historic buildings, has an outdoor courtyard, free city maps, wifi and more.

HOTEL DELUXE
729 SW 15th Ave., 503-219-2094
www.hoteldeluxeportland.com
There's a huge black-and-white still of Alice Faye (I think it's Alice Faye), a big MGM star of the 1930s, gracing the lobby. (Across the room is Cary Grant.) This was built as a hotel in 1912, but hadn't been renovated since the 1940s, until the Provenance group bought it, cleaned it up and reopened in 2006 with a lot of Art Décor furniture and a full-on homage to the Golden Age of the Movies. It's a beautiful property right Downtown, convenient to everything.

HOTEL ROSE
50 SW Morrison St, 503-221-0711
www.hotelroseportland.com
Downtown directly across from Tom McCall Waterfront Park. Modern rooms immaculately maintained. Home to the **H5O Bistro & Bar**, a lively

gathering place around cocktail hour with pretty good food too.

HOTEL MONACO
506 SW Washington St. (at 5th Ave.), 503-222-0001
www.monaco-portland.com
Downtown. A Kimpton property, so you know it's luxe. 4-Diamond Award. Though they welcome pets, they have a whole floor that's hypoallergenic. Some suites. Wine hour in the evening. Free bikes, a fitness center, Spa treatments in their Spa or in-room. Home to **Red Star Tavern & Roast House** (try the smoked Wagyu brisket). Good bar scene at happy hour.

HOTEL VINTAGE PLAZA
422 SW Broadway, 503-228-1212

www.vintageplaza.com
Downtown. Another Kimpton property in an historic restored building. I count 9 different types of rooms you can book here, from large Spa suites to interesting rooms with 45-degree slanted conservatory style windows. (Ask for a "Starlight" room—there are 9 of these on the property.) Free wine tasting in the lobby early evening. The restaurant next door is **Pazzo**, serving Northern Italian cuisine. www.pazzo.com - the **PazzoBar** has a special bar menu that keeps hour busy. (The salumi plate is nice.)

HOTEL ZAGS
515 SW Clay St., 855-523-6914
https://www.thehotelzags.com/
Stylish boutique hotel in downtown, the Modera is ultra-chic, boasting 500 pieces of from Oregon artists decorating its rooms and public spaces, highlighted by Carrara marble, black walnut flooring, sleek

architecture and mod attitude. 24-hour concierge service.

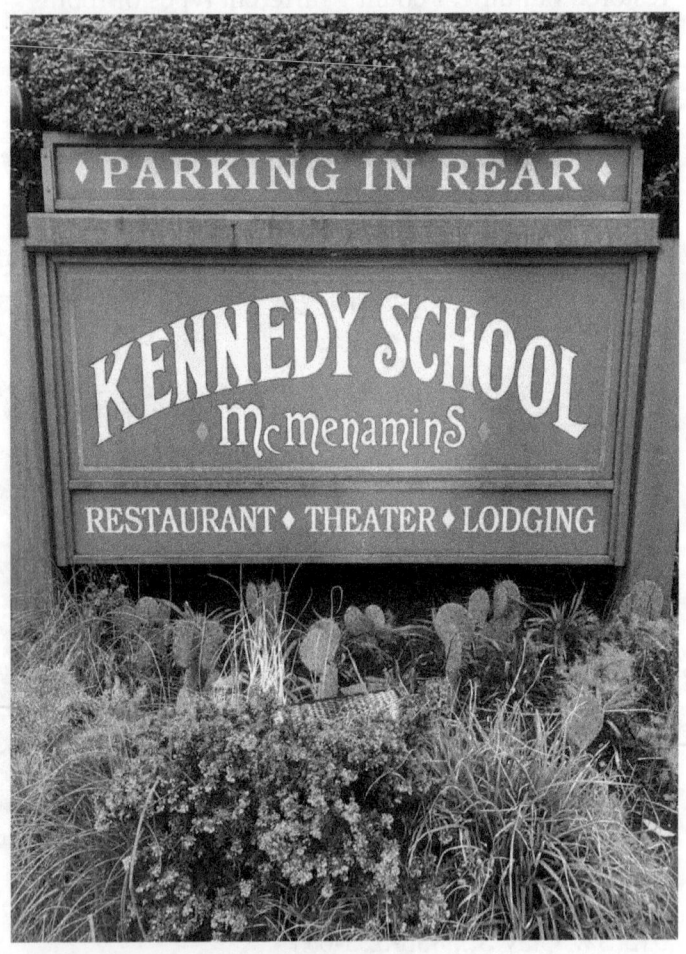

THE KENNEDY SCHOOL
5736 NE 33rd Ave., 503-249-3983
www.mcmenamins.com

A decommissioned elementary school converted into a hotel by the **McMenamin** group who also have several other converted buildings in the Portland area. Each room was made from one-half of an old classroom with items like blackboards, coatrooms, and so on still in place. The hotel has a full restaurant with its own bar and large outdoor patio. The **Courtyard Restaurant** has a turn-of-the-century feel, lots of old dark woods, whimsical lighting fixtures. It's set in the school old cafeteria. Serves breakfast, lunch and dinner. Everything is made on-site. Here are several bars here: the **Concordia Microbrewery, Detention Bar** (smoking allowed), **Honor's Bar** (non-smoking), **Cypress Room** (smoking allowed), and an outdoor soaking pool. Free Wi-Fi and great artwork throughout. There's also a second-run movie theater (free with hotel stay) with a bar/cafe and table service.

MARRIOTT PORTLAND CITY CENTER
520 SW Broadway, 503 226-6300
www.marriott.com/hotels/travel/pdxct-portland-marriott-city-center
Downtown you'll find this newly renovated Marriott property with all the usual amenities. Close to the MAX Light Rail system. 249 rooms.

MCMENAMINS WHITE EAGLE
836 N Russell St., 503-282-6810
www.mcmenamins.com/WhiteEagle
The "formal" name is really **White Eagle Cafe and Rock 'n' Roll Hotel**, and this is because it's not just a

hotel but also the locale for nightly rock 'n roll shows. Quite a scene. The hotel is funky and fun. They offer 11 basic rooms (very cheap) above the music venue and bar.

THE NINES
525 SW Morrison St, Portland, 877-229-9995
www.thenines.com
Located in the former Meier & Frank department store building dating from 1909, this luxury hotel offers beautiful upscale accommodations using a design motif of Tiffany-blue and lots of rich dark woods. There's a bustling happy here on the roof at **Departure**, the rooftop bar & lounge (serving a great menu of Pan-Asian cuisine) that attracts a good looking crowd of locals. You'll get a great view, too, of Mount Hood and Mount St. Helens, or what's left of it after the volcano erupted. Amenities include: Flat-screen TVs and complimentary Wi-Fi, some rooms include breakfast and evening cocktails. Hotel facilities include: several dining options, two bars and 24-hour fitness center.

RIVERPLACE
1510 SW Harbor Way, Portland, 503-228-3233
www.riverplacehotel.com
Downtown Kimpton hotel overlooking the Willamette River with an elegant lobby that matches the elegant rooms upstairs. The design is rustic African—tufted leather headboards, braided rope chairs, lots of tribal art. Amenities include: flat-screen TVs and Wi-Fi (fee). Hotel facilities include:

waterfront bar and grill and meeting rooms. Pet friendly and smoke-free.

SOCIETY HOTEL
203 NW 3rd Ave, Portland, 503-445-0444
www.thesocietyhotel.com
NEIGHBORHOOD: Old Town/Chinatown
Built in 1881 as a boarding house for sailors, this historic hotel offers comfortable hostel style accommodations. Private rooms with shared bathrooms are available. Hotel features: Comfortable

café in the lobby and open-air rooftop deck. Laundry facilities available. Less than a mile from the Portland Art Museum and a 3-minute walk to the train station

SENTINEL HOTEL
614 SW 11th Ave., 503-224-3400
www.sentinelhotel.com
Downtown. Historic 4-star hotel in a restored building dating back to 1909 when it first opened as the Seward Hotel. It was one of America's last "handmade" buildings, with an Arts and Crafts–inspired exterior detailing and interior furnishings. The hotel was restored to its original grandeur in the early 1990s, reopening as the Governor Hotel in 1992. Completely modern amenities. **Jake's Grill** is the in-house eatery featuring Northwest Pacific cuisine heavy on seafood and steaks.

Chapter 4
WHERE TO EAT

DID YOU FIND AN INTERESTING PLACE?
If you discover a place you think I should check out on my next visit, drop me a line, will you? I'll mention your name if I end up listing it.
andrewdelaplaine@mac.com

AVA GENE'S
3377 SE Division St., 971-229-0571
www.avagenes.com

CUISINE: American, Italian
DRINKS: Full Bar
SERVING: Dinner nightly from 5
PRICE RANGE: $$$
Duane Sorenson, who owns Stumptown Coffee, also has this Italian eatery that's noted for its elegance (by Portland standards). Creative dishes like a salad of butter greens topped with melted cheese. Nice salumi selection, crunchy veggies items like snap peas & onion; zucchini, pine nuts, colatura; artichokes, faro and favas; leg of lamb sausages, pork steak, rabbit agnolotti with peas and morels. Really nice place. (There's a 5-course chef's tasting menu I heartily recommend.)

BAMBOO
836 NW 23rd Ave., Portland: 971-229-1925
bamboosushi.com
CUISINE: Japanese, Sushi
DRINKS: Full Bar
SERVING: Dinner daily
PRICE RANGE: $$$
Trendy sushi bar with an emphasis on "eco" cuisine, or so they say. Very lively place. Lots of fun. I don't know how eco friendly a sushi joint can claim to be when some of the fish they sell is near extinction, but what the hell.

BAO BAO DUMPLING HOUSE
133 Spring St, Portland, 207-772-8400
www.baobaodumplinghouse.com
CUISINE: Chinese
DRINKS: Full Bar

SERVING: Lunch & Dinner; closed Mondays & Tuesdays
PRICE RANGE: $$
Small Chinese eatery known for its delicious dumplings. Menu has three sections: cold, bao and hot. Favorites include: Thread Cut Hake and Burdock dumplings. Impressive bar menu of beer, wine, sake, and cocktails.

BIJOU CAFÉ
132 SW 3rd Ave, Portland, 503-222-3187
www.bijoucafepdx.com
CUISINE: French/American (New)
DRINKS: Full Bar
SERVING: Breakfast & Lunch; Dinner only on Fridays
PRICE RANGE: $$
NEIGHBORHOOD: Chinatown
A favorite place for breakfast and jazz dinners (Live jazz every Friday night). Favorites: Hood Canal oyster sandwich, Kale hash and Fried chicken & pancakes. This place uses fresh, local ingredients and mostly organic.

CASTAGNA
1752 SE Hawthorne Blvd, Portland, 503-231-7373
www.castagnarestaurant.com
CUISINE: New American
DRINKS: Full Bar
SERVING: Dinner; closed Mondays
PRICE RANGE: $$$$
Modern minimalist eatery offering a fixed-price menu of "new Northwest" cuisine. The celebrated chef here uses botanicals that grow in a garden close by, as well as oyster emulsions, smoked-beef powders and lots of other original ingredients you don't see anywhere else. Menu changes with the seasons. One of the most interesting menus in Portland. Nice selection of wines.

COOPERS HALL
404 SE 6th Ave, Portland, 503-719-7000

www.coopershall.com
CUISINE: Wine Bar
DRINKS: Full Bar
SERVING: Dinner; closed Sundays
PRICE RANGE: $$
Wine bar situated in a former auto repair shop on the east side that offers over 35 wines on tap. They buy barrels from local wineries and then mix their own blends here on site, so what you drink here you can't buy in stores. Excellent Nosh menu, like the chicken glazed with soy.

CREMA COFFEE & BAKERY
2728 SE Ankeny St, Portland, 503-234-0206
www.cremabakery.com
CUISINE: Bakery
DRINKS: No Booze
SERVING: Breakfast/Lunch/Late afternoon
PRICE RANGE: $$
NEIGHBORHOOD: Southeast Portland/Buckman
Casual eatery with a modern industrial feel serving primarily sandwiches and baked goods. A coffee lover's hangout. Custom cakes & pastries. Free Wi-Fi.

CLYDE COMMON
Ace Hotel
1014 SW Stark St., 503-228-3333
www.clydecommon.com
CUISINE: American
DRINKS: Full Bar
SERVING: Lunch & Dinner; brunch weekends 9-3.
PRICE RANGE: $$
Clyde Common is just as hip as the trendy hotel it's located in, the Ace. It's got a real buzz about it, especially at happy hour. Braised lamb with summer squash; pork with beans and mustard vinaigrette; seared trout with black rice. I'm not a big fan of the communal seating craze, in ample evidence here, but everybody else seems to be OK with it.

DAME
2930 NE Killingsworth St, Portland, 503-227-2669
www.damerestaurant.com

CUISINE: Seafood/American (New)
DRINKS: Full Bar
SERVING: Dinner; closed Tuesday
PRICE RANGE: $$$
NEIGHBORHOOD: Northeast/Concordia/Alberta Arts District
Chic, intimate eatery offering a seasonal menu of creative New American fare. Favorites: Beef tartare and Scallops. Nice wine pairings (mostly natural wines). Simple but creative desserts.

DAVENPORT
2215 E Burnside St, Portland, 503-236-8747
www.davenportpdx.com
CUISINE: Seafood/American (New)
DRINKS: Full Bar
SERVING: Dinner; closed Sun & Mon
PRICE RANGE: $$$
NEIGHBORHOOD: Northeast/Kerns
Warm industrial decorated eatery offering a rotating menu of eclectic American fare. Small plate menu picks: Sliced halibut and Braised pork. Excellent selection of aged wines that are better priced here than they would be at other restaurants.

DEPARTURE RESTAURANT & LOUNGE
Nines Hotel
525 SW Morrison St, Portland, 503-802-5370
www.departureportland.com
CUISINE: Asian Fusion/Korean
DRINKS: Full Bar
SERVING: Dinner
PRICE RANGE: $$$

Popular Pan-Asian restaurant and lounge (crammed at happy hour with a good-looking trendy bunch) with an interior design right out of the *Jetsons* – has an outside patio up on the 15th floor– offering a creative menu of Asian cuisine. Menu favorites include: Smoked Duck Curry and Maguro Karai Honey sushi rolls. Reservations recommended.

DIG A PONY
Central Eastside, 736 SE Grand Ave., 971-279-4409
www.digaponyportland.com
CUISINE: American
DRINKS: Full Bar
SERVING: Dinner-Late Night
PRICE RANGE: $ to $$
Trendy cocktails are the draw in this former diner turned hip hangout. People push up against the horseshow-shaped bar for their favorite. While it's a

restaurant, it's also jumping at night when DJs spin old vinyl. You can see downtown Portland through the big windows looming beyond the Morrison Bridge. Chicken thighs with stewed tomatoes; 4-cheese mac with caramelized onion and jalapeno; sautéed mushrooms with soft egg, shoestring fries.

EAST ENDER
47 Middle St, Portland, 207-879-7669
www.eastenderportland.com
CUISINE: American
DRINKS: Full Bar
SERVING: Lunch & Dinner
PRICE RANGE: $$
The people here started with the popular Small Ax Food Truck but finally opened a permanent eatery. Popular place with a menu of American classics, including perhaps the best burger in all of Portland (and that's saying something). Menu picks include: Lobster melt and the Smoked burger. Nice bar menu including crafted cocktails and local beers.

EURO TRASH
Corner of SW 10th & Washington
www.eurotrashcart.com
CUISINE: Modern European, Food Truck
DRINKS: No Booze
SERVING: Lunch
PRICE RANGE: $
Prawn baguette (grilled curried prawns with a cold cilantro curry coconut slaw); Piri Piri chicken, grilled chicken, bacon and capers and 5 or 6 other real delicacies are served out of this gourmet food truck. (You'd HATE to own a restaurant across the street from where this guy parks.) The food is so good and so cheap it's ridiculous.

FIRESIDE
801 NW 23rd Ave, Portland, 503-477-9505
www.pdxfireside.com
CUISINE: American (New)
DRINKS: Full Bar

SERVING: Lunch & Dinner; closed Sunday night
PRICE RANGE: $$
Housed in the former Music Millennium building, this new upscale eatery offers a creative menu of Northwest cuisine using lots of fresh, organic locally sourced foods. Menu favorites include: Braised Lamb sandwich and Steak salad. Nice cocktail menu. Great choice for weekend brunch.

FRIED EGG I'M IN LOVE
3549 SE Hawthorne Blvd, Portland, 503-610-3447
www.friedegglove.com
CUISINE: Breakfast/Sandwiches
DRINKS: Beer & Wine
SERVING: Breakfast/Lunch
PRICE RANGE: $
NEIGHBORHOOD: Southeast/Hawthorne/Sunnyside

Hot breakfast spot offering an impressive variety of egg sandwiches. Basically a food truck with a few picnic tables. Gluten-free, vegetarian, and vegan options available. Beverages: coffee, mimosas, beer and cider. They also serve hot and cold Stumptown Coffee, as well as mimosas, beer, and cider.

THE FRYING SCOTSMAN
SW 9th Ave. & SW Alder St., 503-706-3841
http://the-frying-scotsman-portland.sites.beta.tablehero.com/

CUISINE: Fish & Chips, Scottish
DRINKS: No Booze
SERVING: Lunch
PTICE RANGE: $

Authentic fish & chips the specialty here. Chef James King comes from Ayrshire on the west coast of Scotland. He uses a family recipe handed down over the years for the lightly breaded quality fish he cooks.

FULLER'S RESTAURANT
136 NW 9th Ave, Portland, 503-222-5608
No Website
CUISINE: Breakfast
DRINKS: Full Bar
SERVING: Breakfast/Lunch; closed Mondays
PRICE RANGE: $
NEIGHBORHOOD: Pearl District

Old-school lunch counter in a 960s diner serving basic menu of American comfort food. Favorites: Any of the omelets and their unique version of the Pig in a Blanket (sausage wrapped in a German pancake). Delicious milkshakes.

GRAVY
3957 N. Mississippi Ave., Portland: 503-287-8800
http://gravyrestaurant.com/
CUISINE: American
DRINKS: Full bar
SERVING: Daily breakfast and brunch
PRICE RANGE: $$
Lively place with lots of young people, artists, creative types in for good cheap food and large portions. Breakfast items excel: biscuits & gravy; Monte Cristo with French toast; banana pecan

oatmeal brulee; chicken fried steak & hash browns; smoked salmon hash.

HA & VL
2738 SE 82nd Ave. #102, 503-772-0103
http://mrgan.com/havl/
CUISINE: Vietnamese
DRINKS: No booze
SERVING: Wed – Mon breakfast and lunch, Tues closed
PRICE RANGE: $
For bahn mi & pho lovers, this is the place. Authentic Vietnamese food. Also great sandwiches. It's completely hidden in a little strip mall, so look for it.

HAN OAK
511 NE 24th Ave, Portland, 971-255-0032
www.hanoakpdx.com
CUISINE: Korean/American (New)
DRINKS: Full Bar
SERVING: Dinner; closed Tues - Thurs
PRICE RANGE: $$$
NEIGHBORHOOD: Northeast/Kerns
Chic Korean eatery offering an upscale dining experience with tasting menus & drink pairings, plus noodle & dumpling nights. You can watch t the cooks hand-cut noodles and dumplings in the open kitchen. Favorites: Beef short rib and super stuffed dumplings. Prix-fixe menu. Popular choice for Sunday brunch.

HEADWATERS
The Heathman Hotel
1001 SW Broadway, Portland, 503-790-7752

www.headwaterspdx.com
CUISINE: Seafood
DRINKS: Full Bar
SERVING: Dinner
PRICE RANGE: $$$
NEIGHBORHOOD: Southwest/Downtown
Upscale historic hotel eatery focusing on seafood with a French flair. Menu picks: Seared diver scallops, smoked fish with a herring schmear, halibut en papillote and Albacore and green bean salad. Not into fish? They serve a tasty burger with fries. Dessert favorite: Honey cake with lavender ice cream.

HUBER'S CAFÉ
411 SW 3rd Ave., 503-228-5686
www.hubers.com
CUISINE: American
DRINKS: Full Bar
SERVING: Lunch-Dinner
PRICE RANGE: $$

With the huge emphasis you find in Portland on "farm to table" cuisine and on "artisanal" foods and pickled this and pickled that, it's fun to find a place where the reputation is based on turkey dinners and flaming Spanish coffee served tableside. The traditional house specialty is served with sage dressing, fresh mashed potatoes and homemade cranberry sauce. Baked sugar-glazed ham dinners also. They have interesting takes on turkey: turkey piccata, turkey enchiladas, turkey mushroom pie, things like that. There's an Art Deco skylight in the historic Oregon Pioneer Building where Huber's is located that's a treat to see.

IMPERIAL
410 SW Broadway, 503-228-7222
www.imperialpdx.com
CUISINE: American
DRINKS: Full Bar

SERVING: Breakfast-Lunch & Dinner
PRICE RANGE: $$$
Part of Russian-born Chef Vitaly Paley's empire in Portland. Here you can expect hearty comfort food with a twist: duck meatballs, grilled lamb tongue, trout (or halibut) a la plancha, fried rabbit (which I rarely see, but love). Vitaly has a 6-foot wide wood-fired grill which produces things like an organic half chicken; grilled lamb chops; dry aged rib eye; quail; sausages; and a bone-in pork chop that's delicately mouthwatering.

KACHKA
720 SE Grand Ave, Portland, 503-235-0059
www.kachkapdx.com
CUISINE: Russian
DRINKS: Full Bar
SERVING: Dinner
PRICE RANGE: $$
Bustling eatery serving refined Russian fare. I happen to love herring in all its many forms. Here, they have it all. They focus on *zakuski,* which means serving shots of vodka with appetizers like smoked fish spread, picked veggies and stuffed eggs. Sour cream is used in many dishes, to excellent effect (like the wonderful braised chicken thighs with potatoes, porcini mushrooms, lots of garlic and dried cherries). Other favorites include: Herring Under a Fur Coat (a sort of 7-layer dip popular in Russia), *cholodetz* (beef shank, veal feet terrine served with hard boiled eggs in aspic) and Beef Dumplings loaded down with sour cream. It goes without saying their selection of

Russian vodkas is vast. (Do you know that Russian is the third most-spoken language in Portland?)

LARDO
East Side: 1212 SE Hawthorne, 503-234-7786 (Central Eastside)
West Side: 1205 SW Washington St., 503-241-2490
www.lardosandwiches.com
CUISINE: Sandwiches
DRINKS: Full Bar
SERVING: Lunch-Dinner
PRICE RANGE: $

Some of the best sandwiches in Portland. Eggplant parm; pork meatball Banh Mi; smoked Coppa Cubano; sausage, egg & cheese—and here's my favorite, their double burger with beef from the Cascades topped with cheddar cheese, "porkstrami" and Lardo sauce. (At presstime this astounding creation was only $9.) Great selection of local beers to wash all these sandwiches down. (But you have to bring your own Lipitor.)

LAURELHURST MARKET
3155 E Burnside St, Portland, 503-206-3097
www.laurelhurstmarket.com
CUISINE: Steakhouse
DRINKS: Full Bar
SERVING: Lunch & Dinner
PRICE RANGE: $$$

Combination butcher shop and steakhouse with a meat-themed menu. Great cuts of meat and delicious sandwiches.

LAURETTA JEAN'S
3402 SE Division St., 503-235-3119
www.laurettajean.com
CUISINE: Cafés, Bakeries
DRINKS: Full Bar
SERVING: Breakfast-Lunch
PRICE RANGE: $
Stop in for a slice at this charming little place. A slice of pie, not pizza! Blackberry raspberry streusel, blueberry rhubarb, coconut cream, many others. Seasonal quiche is also served. Great place to get a bacon, egg & cheese biscuit for breakfast.

LE PIGEON
738 E Burnside St, Portland, 503-546-8796
www.lepigeon.com
CUISINE: French/American (New)
DRINKS: Beer & Wine Only
SERVING: Dinner
PRICE RANGE: $$$
Great menu of French-inspired cuisine served at communal tables by a James Beard Foundation Award winner. Expect unusual dishes mixing complicated flavors, like rabbit and eel terrine. Favorites include: Ratatouille (very good) and Beef Cheeks. Nice menu of wines and beers.

MAURICE LUNCHONETTE
921 SW Oak St, Portland, 503-224-9921
www.mauricepdx.com
CUISINE: French/Pastries
DRINKS: Beer & Wine Only
SERVING: Breakfast, Lunch & Dinner
PRICE RANGE: $$
This really charming little French kitchen offers a tasty assortment of pastries and French cuisine in a spanking all-white room with lots of lovely touches: handwritten menus, fresh flowers. At first glance, you're cynical, but after 10 minutes, you're completely won over by the loveliness of this place. Try the fresh chicken paté topped by pickled mustard seeds. I urge you to try the lemon-soufflé pudding cake. I never had anything like it before. Simply wonderful. This place feels like a café in France.

They even have over 30 varieties of vermouth. Now, *that's* French!

McMENAMINS KENNEDY SCHOOL
5736 NE 33rd Ave., 503-249-3983
www.mcmenamins.com
CUISINE: American
DRINKS: Full Bar
SERVING: Breakfast, Lunch & Dinner
PRICE RANGE: $$

A decommissioned elementary school converted into a hotel by the **McMenamin** group who also have several other converted buildings in the Portland area. Each room was made from one-half of an old classroom with items like blackboards, coatrooms, and so on still in place. The hotel has a full restaurant with its own bar and large outdoor patio. The **Courtyard Restaurant** has a turn-of-the-century feel, lots of old dark woods, whimsical lighting fixtures. It's set in the school old cafeteria. Serves breakfast, lunch and dinner. Everything is made on-site. Here are several bars here: the **Concordia Microbrewery, Detention Bar** (smoking allowed), **Honor's Bar** (non-smoking), **Cypress Room** (smoking allowed), and an outdoor soaking pool. Free Wi-Fi and great artwork throughout. There's also a second-run movie theater (free with hotel stay) with a bar/cafe and table service.

MULTNOMAH WHISKEY LIBRARY
1124 SW Alder St, Portland, 503-954-1381
https://mwlpdx.com/
CUISINE: Small Plates

DRINKS: Full Bar
SERVING: Dinner; closed Sundays
PRICE RANGE: $$$
A cozy upstairs lounge that offers a menu of over 1,000 spirts. Menu of small plates available for noshing (fried Kentucky quail with a smoked blue-cheese biscuit) but most savants come here for the serious drinking. Comfortable atmosphere with couches, tables, and bar seating. Reservations recommended.

NED LUDD
3925 NE Martin Luther King Jr Blvd, Portland, 503-288-6900
www.nedluddpdx.com
CUISINE: American (New)
DRINKS: Full Bar
SERVING: Dinner, Lunch on weekends
PRICE RANGE: $$$
Small rustic designed eatery (the plates are all mismatched on purpose, that sort of thing) with a menu of inventive New American cuisine – many items cooked in the wood burning oven employing cherry and maple woods. I loved the roasted Idaho trout served with charred Brussels sprouts with lemon and feta. You'll need reservations needed for dinner unless you get there early.

NORANEKO
1430 SE Water Ave, Portland, 503-238-6356
www.noranekoramen.com
CUISINE: Ramen/Noodles/Sandwiches
DRINKS: Full Bar

SERVING: Lunch/Dinner
PRICE RANGE: $$
NEIGHBORHOOD: Central Eastside/Hosford-Abernethy
Hipster eatery known for their ramen but also serves notable Japanese ramen soups, dumplings & kimchi. Small place with little wooden tables. Popular with the late-night crowd.

OLYMPIA PROVISIONS
Northwest: 1632 NW Thurman St., 503-894-8136
Southeast: 107 SE Washington St., 503-954-3663
https://www.olympiaprovisions.com/
CUISINE: American
DRINKS: Full Bar
SERVING: Lunch-Dinner
PRICE RANGE: $$
Olympic Provisions is home to Oregon's first USDA-approved salumeria, established in 2009. Both locations operate as European-style restaurants,

bustling neighborhood delis, and onsite meat-curing facilities, where salumist and owner Elias Cairo carefully crafts "American Charcuterie" using the highest quality local ingredients. So you simply have to have a charcuterie board here—they make it all. Other interesting items: spit roasted pork shoulder

crepinette; crispy skinned salmon; octopus terrine; pan-roasted halibut. They also have the best rotisserie chicken in town: it's crispy on the outside and so moist on the inside. But get that on your second visit. First time, stick with the meats here. They're out of this world.

OX
2225 NE MLK Jr. Blvd., Portland: 503-284-3366
oxpdx.com
CUISINE: Argentine
DRINKS: Full bar
SERVING: Tues – Sun dinner only, Mon closed

PRICE RANGE: $$$
Wonderful place (very small) where they'll cook a whole lamb if you want them to. If that's a little more than your party requires, you can settle for the perfectly delectable grilled lamb heart over arugula as a starter, moving on to the lamb shoulder chop or the house-made chorizo. While they are inspired by Argentine wood-grilling techniques (and the delicious flavors those techniques produce), they aren't slaves to it, as lots of creative dishes testify. They have lots of Argentine favorites like blood sausage, but there are well-executed dishes that will appeal to the non-meat eater, like Alaskan halibut with toasted garlic. Simple and lovely.

MEE-SEN THAI EATERY
3924 N Mississippi Ave., Portland: 503-445-1909
https://meesenthaiportland.com
CUISINE: Thai
DRINKS: Full bar

SERVING: Daily lunch and dinner
PRICE RANGE: $$
If you have a thing for noodles and don't want to spend a day on a plane to Bangkok, get your butt down here. Very authentic cuisine. Get the fried egg on top of the garlicky stir-fry.

PALEY'S PLACE
1204 NW 21st Ave., 503-243-2403
www.paleysplace.net
CUISINE: French; Northwest Pacific
DRINKS: Full Bar
SERVING: Dinner
PRICE RANGE: $$$
Start with the excellent and flavorful charcuterie here: wonderfully different items like rabbit bologna, braised goat terrine, confit of beef tongue. Move on to

the sweet corn and duck egg ravioli; prawns a la plancha; crispy sweetbreads. (The side dishes merit special attention.) Namesake eatery of **Chef Vitaly Paley**, who also has the **Imperial** and **Paley's Penny Diner**.

PINE STATE BISCUITS
1100 SE Division St, Portland, 503-236-3346
www.pinestatebiscuits.com
CUISINE: Southern/Sandwiches
DRINKS: Full Bar
SERVING: Breakfast & Lunch; Dinner Thurs - Sun
PRICE RANGE: $

As the name implies, this place specializes in comfort food. It's a small place and they expect you to bus your own table but the food is tasty – especially the fresh baked buttermilk biscuits. Menu favorites include: Reggie Deluxe – made from fried chicken, bacon, gravy and egg and BBQ Pork.

POK POK
3226 SE Division St., 503-232-1387
www.pokpokpdx.com
CUISINE: Thai
DRINKS: Full Bar
SERVING: Lunch-Dinner
PRICE RANGE: $$

Long before Chef Andy Ricker hit the international map by opening a Pok Pok in Brooklyn, he was dishing out innovative cuisine here in Portland. The 2011 James Beard Best Chef Northwest serves up some excellent Thai food. Try the Sai Ua Samun Phrai (Chiang Mai sausage with herbs, Burmese curry powder and aromatics). He sells a lot of noodle dishes, of course, but the specialty of the house is Kai Yaang (rotisserie chicken stuffed with lemongrass, garlic, pepper and cilantro). You've never had rotisserie chicken like this. Note: this Thai food is based on recipes found in the north part of the country, not the usual southern recipes served in most U.S. Thai restaurants.

THE PORTLAND BOTTLE SHOP
7960 SE 13th Ave., Portland: 503-232-5202
pdxbottleshop.com
Monthly dinners are held in this charming little place, cooked by local chefs featuring small-batch wines and locally made charcuterie. Always a treat for about $60 a head. Get on their email list in advance so you're the first to know. These great events sell out quickly. You'll really get a "local" experience.

RENATA
626 SE Main St, Portland, 503-954-2708
www.renatapdx.com
CUISINE: Italian
DRINKS: Full Bar
SERVING: Dinner
PRICE RANGE: $$$
NEIGHBORHOOD: Southeast/Buckman
Grand upscale Italian eatery offering a fine-dining experience. Favorites: Canestri and Halibut. Known for their freshly made pastas and pizzas. Nice selection of Italian desserts including panna cotta and gelato.

RINGSIDE
2165 W. Burnside St., Portland: 503-223-1513
14021 NE Glisan, Portland: 503-255-0750
ringsidesteakhouse.com
CUISINE: Steakhouse, Seafood
DRINKS: Full bar
SERVING: Daily dinner
PRICE RANGE: $$$
This place reminds me of the steakhouses of my youth, like Hy Uchitel's Place of Steak in North Bay Village in Miami where all the lower-level Mafia guys would hang out along with celebrities and high-rollers. James Beard once said the onion rings here were "the best I ever had." In a town where seafood reigns supreme, sometimes you want a good old-fashioned steak. Get it here. You can beat this place. Been here forever. Go for one of their bone-in cuts, aged on premises. The bar here is a great place to

hang out. It's really dark in here. The bartender sits in a pit surrounded by portraits of boxers. So cool.

SLAB
25 Preble St, Portland, 207-245-3088
www.slabportland.com
CUISINE: Pizza/Italian
DRINKS: Full Bar
SERVING: Lunch & Dinner; closed Sundays
PRICE RANGE: $$
If you've never had a slab, then you're in for a treat. Delicious Sicilian slab pizza and meatball sandwiches. Casual eatery with an outdoor patio.

TASTY n SONS
3808 N. Williams (Suite C), 503-621-1400
580 SW 12 Ave., 503-621-9251
www.tastynsons.com/
CUISINE: American
DRINKS: Full Bar
SERVING: Breakfast (from 9); lunch, brunch, dinner
PRICE RANGE: $$

For starters: Low country hush puppies; anchovy fish & chips; clams with chorizo; radicchio with lardons, manchego and chopped 6-minute egg. Just the best in meats: Iberico pork skirt steak, lamb chops from Anderson Ranch; pork Jagerschnitzel.

TEOTE AREPERIA
1615 SE 12th Ave, Portland, 971-888-5281
www.teotepdx.com
CUISINE: Latin American
DRINKS: Full Bar
SERVING: Lunch & Dinner
PRICE RANGE: $$
NEIGHBORHOOD: Southeast/Hosford-Abernethy
Hip Latin American eatery with a menu of creative street fare. Menu pick: Slow-cooked shredded chicken. Try the arepas – not a main course but it could be. Gluten-free options. Order downstairs then go upstairs to dine or on the patio where there's a fire pit.

TORO BRAVO
120 NE Russell St., 503-281-4464
www.torobravopdx.com
CUISINE: Tapas Bars, Spanish; American
DRINKS: Full Bar
SERVING: Dinner
PRICE RANGE: $$
Menu changes daily, since it's built around seasonal ingredients, but expect tapas plates like fried Spanish anchovies with fennel and lemon; Basque Piperade with duck egg; grilled artichokes with espelette and honey; sautéed snap peas with ham; empanada with

tomato-braised pork. Also squid ink pasta with hazelnuts, anchovy syrup; noodles with bacon and sea urchin; roasted eggplant with lamb ragu.

TUSK
2448 East Burnside St, Portland, 503-894-8082
www.tuskpdx.com
CUISINE: Middle Eastern
DRINKS: Full Bar
SERVING: Dinner/Lunch on Sat & Sun
PRICE RANGE: $$
NEIGHBORHOOD: Southeast/Buckman
There's a picture of Keith Richards above the bar wearing a Speedo in a pool. The name Tusk comes from a Fleetwood Mac album. I always associate Portland with a dark and dreary ambience, but that idea is nowhere to be seen in this fun, lively, bright place. Popular Middle Eastern eatery (using local ingredients) serving bold and adventurous food like Man'oushe (porcinis, squash blossoms and cheese curds). They have a tasting menu called the Magic Carpet Ride that allows you to taste wonderful mezze, veggies cooked to perfection, skewers of meat, different dips, cracked olives, Egyptian dukka-flavored items, housemade pita to mop up juices, hummus using chickpeas from a farm in Washington State, feta cheese made with 100% sheep's milk topped with za'atar and rose petals, lamb, local grains, a little bit of everything. Other Menu picks: Chicken skewers and Crispy bread with chicken curry. Try the delicious Tahini soft serve for dessert. Reservations recommended.

WATER AVENUE COFFEE
1028 SE Water Ave., 503-808-7084
www.wateravenuecoffee.com
Central Eastside. Here's you'll find a hip young crowd (many on bikes, you'll notice from the full bike rack outside) who come because the coffee is so good. They're dedicated to micro-roasting craft coffees. The bar and counter seating comes from a 100-year-old reclaimed tree (it's a type of fir, I was told when I inquired). The customers are almost as covered in tattoos as the knowledgeable baristas.

Chapter 5
NIGHTLIFE

DID YOU FIND AN INTERESTING PLACE?
If you discover a place you think I should check out on my next visit, drop me a line, will you? I'll mention your name if I end up listing it.
andrewdelaplaine@mac.com

AMBONNAY CHAMPAGNE BAR
107 SE Washington St., 503-575-4861

www.ambonnaybar.com
Small romantic wine bar—well, a sparkling wine bar. Here you'll find a wide array of Champagne and other sparklers poured by the glass or the bottle. Sommelier David Speer runs the show. Unless you plan to sit around and drink Champagne all night, this places make a good romantic stop on your way somewhere else.)"Ambonnay" is a region in the Champagne District.)

BAILEY'S TAPROOM
213 SW Broadway, 503-295-1004
www.baileystaproom.com
Downtown. The focus here is on the endlessly rotating tap beer emphasizing the products Oregon breweries, which as you well know there are about a thousand.

CLINTON STREET THEATER
2522 S.E. Clinton St., Portland: 503-897-0744
clintonsttheater.com

Fun cinema where they show cult favorites like "The Rocky Horror Picture Show." Also runs rare documentaries. Dilapidated seats, but they sell beer on tap.

DEVILS POINT
5305 SE Foster Rd, 503-774-4513
www.devilspointbar.com
Adult entertainment in probably the best strip club in Oregon. Don't miss the Fire Dance.

DRIFTWOOD ROOM
Hotel Deluxe
729 SW 15th Ave., 503-219-2094
hoteldeluxeportland.com
This used to be the Mallory Hotel, but I like the current name because it sounds so downmarket. The bar in here is like a throwback to the 1950s. They cleaned up the hotel a few years ago, but they left this gem mostly intact. Come in here to go back in time.

And be a grown up when you come here. Get a GIN martini, not vodka.

EASTBURN
1800 E Burnside St., 503-236-2876
www.theeastburn.com
CUISINE: American
DRINKS: Full Bar
SERVING: Dinner
PRICE RANGE: $$
Although this is really a restaurant, I've got it here in nightlife because it's got that kind of feel to it. They have a massive patio here (retractable roof in summer). There are those old-fashioned swing-sets you used to see on Grandma's porch (well, my Grandma's porch) that are fun. In the tables they have little pit fires, which throw off some heat in often chilly Portland. Best choices for food: Tuscan white bean spread; steak salad; rack of wild boar ribs; mac & cheese. EastBurn has over a dozen craft beers on tap; selection changes almost every day.

GROUND KONTROL CLASSIC ARCADE
115 NW 5th Ave, 503-796-9364
www.groundkontrol.com
Some 60 classic video games and 27 pinball machines.

HOLLYWOOD THEATRE
4122 N.E. Sandy Blvd., Portland: 503-493-1128
hollywoodtheatre.org

A 1,500 seat Art Deco gem where the non-profit Film Action Oregon group shows indie films. Note the ornate marquee.

HOLOCENE
1001 SE Morrison St, 503-239-7639
www.holocene.org
Dance club and lounge. Has a small but good bar menu with better quality than most.

LOW BROW LOUNGE
1036 NW Hoyt St., 503-226-0200
http://lowbrowlounge.com
A great dive bar where you'll hear a lot of garage rock. Don't forget to order the tater tots with lots of ketchup. (I'm serious.) While it's been pointed out before that the staff doesn't give a damn about you, that's hardly the point. Once you come here, you'll care about this place, although you might wonder why they bothered putting the word "lounge" in their

name when it's just a mildewed dump with lots of wonderful character. (They have a lot of other bar food, by the way, like the fried shrimp basket with smoked tartar sauce.)

REEL M INN
2430 SE Division St., Portland: 503-231-3880
https://www.facebook.com/pages/Reel-M-Inn/120469364632166
One of Portland's best dive bars. Get a can of Rainier Beer and order some of the best fried chicken in Portland. You'll find a colorful crowd range from homeless bums to bikers to cops to artists and other hipsters.

TEARDROP COCKTAIL LOUNGE
1015 NW Everett St, 503-445-8109
www.teardroplounge.com
Pearl District. It's not about beer here. It's about the art of mixology. Fancy drinks concoctions made with the finest ingredients.

VALENTINE'S
232 S.W. Ankeny St., Portland: 503-248-1600
www.valentinespdx.com
Though a hip crowd hangs out here in this high-ceilinged bar, once the DJ cranks it up, things chill out.

Chapter 6
WHAT TO SEE & DO

DID YOU FIND AN INTERESTING PLACE?
If you discover a place you think I should check out on my next visit, drop me a line, will you? I'll mention your name if I end up listing it.
andrewdelaplaine@mac.com

BREWERIES
Portland is known internationals for the proliferation of microbreweries. I've heard that the growth of this little industry dates to the 1980s when state law was changed to allow consumption of beer on brewery

premises. So not only were the brewers brewing, the brewers served what they brewed.

There are some 60 of these microbreweries. That's right, 60 or more. Some visitors come here exclusively to taste the dozens of different brews available and festivals celebrate the local industry. (No other city in the world has so many breweries, including Cologne, Germany.)

The **McMenamin brothers** own about half of them, though they own many more in other cities in the region, maybe 65 in all. (These guys installed breweries in historically significant building, like old cinemas, that otherwise would have been demolished.)

Other notable Portland brewers include **BridgePort, Hair of the Dog,** and **Hopworks Urban Brewery.**

GIGANTIC BREWING COMPANY
5224 SE 26th Ave., Portland: 503-208-3416
giganticbrewing.com
They have a very commodious tasting room here in this industrial chic brewery opened by two of the best brewers in the Northwest, Ben Love and Van Havig.

GROUND KONTROL CLASSIC ARCADE
115 NW 5th Ave, 503-796-9364
www.groundkontrol.com
Futuristic two-story arcade filled with vintage video games and pinball machines. Here you'll find over 60 classic video games and 27 pinball machines along with a full-service bar – after 5 p.m. The venue hosts

comedy shows, trivia nights, game tournaments, and karaoke. Menu of light fare.

HOYT ARBORETUM
4000 SW Fairview Blvd. (on the western side of Washington Park), 503-865-8733
www.hoytarboretum.org
A large arboretum with paved trails of varying lengths and over 1,000 species of trees and plants in a natural setting. Free.

INTERNATIONAL ROSE TEST GARDENS
400 SW Kingston Ave (10 min. on Washington Park Shuttle from Washington Park MAX) 503-823-3636
www.portlandoregon.gov
The largest rose test garden in the U.S., perched on a hill overlooking Downtown and with thousands of roses planted in every possible way: rows, bushes and vines. Best to come between May and July, when it gets fragrant because everything's in bloom. There are free guided tours by volunteer gardeners at 1PM during the summer months. Free.

McCALL WATERFRONT PARK
SW Harrison St and NW Glisan St, 503-823-7529
This is a stunning riverfront park that seems to go on forever. Here's where locals come to run, sunbathe, cycle, or just walk. You'll get great views of the whole town while you watch the rowers zip by on practice sessions. In summer, it seems like there's some kind of festival every week. And there's a market every Saturday that has to be on your list of things to do. Great browsing. A perfect example of

Portland's commitment to a "green" world, this park is named after Governor **Tom McCall**. He was a visionary planner who led the effort to rip up the old railway and return the Willamette Riverfront to pedestrian use. The park has cherry trees and several monuments.

NEW DEAL DISTILLERY
Central Eastside, 900 SE Salmon, 503-234-2513
www.newdealdistillery.com
New Deal makes high quality, craft-distilled spirits (mainly vodkas and gins), inspired by the DIY spirit of Portland. All their artisanal vodkas are made locally in small batches with Bull Run water and natural and organic ingredients, sourced locally whenever possible. Tasting Room is open Wednesday – Friday 1-4, but check to make sure hours are the same.

OAKS AMUSEMENT PARK CAROUSEL
7805 SE Oaks Park Way, 503-233-5777

www.oakspark.com
This carousel is over 100 years old and is located in this amusement part on the east bank of the Willamette River. The various animals (including a cat, dragon, zebra and kangaroo) were carved by Italian and German woodworkers. Other things to do here: mini golf, other rides, bumper cars, and a very good roller rink (with classes if you want them).

OREGON HISTORICAL SOCIETY
1200 SW Park Ave. (across from the Portland Art Museum), 503-222-1741
www.ohs.org
Lots of artifacts and exhibits on the history of the state as well as rotating exhibits that come in on a variety of subjects. Has 6 or 7 exhibits running at one time.

OREGON MUSEUM OF SCIENCE AND INDUSTRY -- OMSI
1945 SE Water Ave., 503-797-4000
www.omsi.edu
OMSI is great for kids, with hundreds of hands-on activities with a particular emphasis on technology and earth sciences; you can spend a full rainy day here and not get bored. Moored in the river just outside is the "USS Blueback," an old Navy submarine which is open for tours (separate ticket required). There's also a planetarium and an IMAX theater which requires separate admission, but you can view the IMAX projector in operation without paying for the movie ticket.

OREGON ZOO
4001 SW Canyon Rd. (on the southern side of Washington Park), 503-226-1561
www.oregonzoo.org
A good-sized zoo with Pacific Northwest animals, a primate house, and an Africa area, as well as a large Asian Elephant exhibit and breeding area, which is noteworthy among zoos.

PIONEER COURTHOUSE SQUARE
701 SW 6th Ave, Portland, 503-223-1613
www.thesquarepdx.org
This is the central plaza in Downtown Portland, a big gathering spot that's popular with tourists and locals alike. Notable features of the park are a cascading waterfall fountain, chess boards, and the **Weather Machine**, a machine that predicts the weather every day at noon. Many other sculptures and art elements surround the square, including **Kvinneakt**, the bronze statue of a nude woman that's otherwise known as the

"Expose Yourself to Art" statue after a popular poster featuring a flasher (former Mayor Bud Clark) facing this work. Free.

PITTOCK MANSION
3229 NW Pittock Dr., Portland: 503-823-3623
pittockmansion.org
Modest admission fee.

A thousand feet above the city's skyline is this monument to Portland's transformation from a small hick lumber town to a city of major international prominence.

It all started English-born Henry Lewis Pittock journeyed on a wagon train from Pennsylvania to Oregon in 1853 where, at the young age of 19, and in his own words, "barefoot and penniless," he began working for Thomas Jefferson Dryer's Weekly Oregonian newspaper.

In 1860, at the age of 26, he married 15-year-old Georgiana Martin Burton of Missouri. Six years prior, Georgiana had crossed the plains from Keokuk, Iowa to Oregon Territory with her parents. Georgiana's father E.M. Burton was a flour mill owner and one of early Portland's well known building contractors.

PORTLAND AERIAL TRAM
3303 SW Bond Ave., (in South Waterfront, at the southern end of the streetcar line)
503-865-TRAM (8726)
www.gobytram.com
Trams depart every 6 minutes for the 3-minute ride (at 20 MPH). This aerial tram, which is part of the Portland public transportation system, was deemed the best way to connect the South Waterfront neighborhood to the Oregon Health Sciences University campus on a hill to the west. The tram is sleek and offers an excellent view of Downtown and

the surrounding area, with splendid views of the mountains on a clear day.

PORTLAND ART MUSEUM
1219 SW Park Ave., 503-226-2811
www.portlandartmuseum.org
Has several outstanding collections and is regularly updated by moving exhibits. It is an expansive museum where on could easily spend an entire afternoon. With trolley and MAX stops nearby, as well as several bus lines,, it is easily accessible by public transportation. The Whitsell Auditorium in the basement of the museum is where the **Northwest Film Center** - www.nwfilm.org - hosts film screenings.

PORTLAND CHILDREN'S MUSEUM
4015 SW Canyon Rd. (on the southern side of Washington Park), Portland, 503-223-6500
www.portlandcm.org
Lots of interactive exhibits designed for kids.

PORTLAND JAPANESE GARDEN
611 SW Kingston Dr. (across from the Rose Test Gardens), 503-223-1321
www.japanesegarden.com
A haven of tranquil beauty which has been called one of the most authentic Japanese gardens outside of Japan. It's got hilly terrain offering superb views of Downtown. In the fall, you'll see very vibrant yellows and cinnamon colors sprouting from the Japanese maples. An expansion added a cultural village that was designed by the famous architect Kengo Kuma.

PORTLANDIA
1120 SW 5th Ave. (W side of Portland Building)
Looming over the west entrance of the Portland Building is the second-largest hammered-copper statue in the U.S. (after the Statue of Liberty); a classical sculpture of a woman bearing a trident, crouching over the entryway and reaching down to welcome visitors. For its sheer size, it's surprisingly easy to miss, so keep your eyes peeled for the postmodern building painted in red, blue, and tan.

ROGUE ALES
1339 NW Flanders St, Portland: 503-222-5910
rogue.com
A brewery worth a visit.

SAPPORO BELL
777 NE Martin Luther King Jr. Blvd. (at the entrance to the Oregon Convention Center)
Sapporo, Japan—Portland's Sister City—gave this huge friendship bell to Portland.

WASHINGTON PARK
4033 Southwest Canyon Road, 503-319-0999
www.explorewashingtonpark.org/exploring
Washington Park is a classic urban park, sprawling over about 140 acres and with a whole bunch of trails that take you between the strands of trees, around the hills and through the canyons, a park so large it can be easy to get lost without a map. In addition to the many attractions located here, it also contains memorials for the Korean and Vietnam Wars, the Holocaust, the Lewis and Clark Expedition, and has beautiful vistas of Portland and Mount Hood. The MAX red and blue lines can take you to the park; the station is located at the south end of the park, outside the World Forestry Center and the Oregon Zoo entrance.

WORLD FORESTRY CENTER DISCOVERY MUSEUM
4033 SW Canyon Road (on the southern side of the park), 503-319-0999
www.worldforestry.org
Built like a giant log cabin, this museum is devoted to the science and cultural impact of Pacific Northwest forests.

Chapter 7
SHOPPING & SERVICES

DID YOU FIND AN INTERESTING PLACE?
If you discover a place you think I should check out on my next visit, drop me a line, will you? I'll mention your name if I end up listing it.
andrewdelaplaine@mac.com

There's lots of great shopping to be found in Portland.

Popular areas are **Downtown Portland**, **Nob Hill** (NW 21st & 23rd Avenues), the **Pearl District,** the **Lloyd District** and **Hawthorne Avenue** for its vintage stores.

Major department stores Downtown include **Nordstrom**, **Macy's**, and **H&M**.

The major malls in the metropolitan area include **Lloyd Center**, **Washington Square**, **Clackamas Town Center**, **Westfield Vancouver**, **Bridgeport Village** and **Pioneer Place**.

And don't overlook the **Portland Saturday Market,** www.portlandsaturdaymarket.com, which is a town bazaar-like environment where many kinds of goods are sold from Artisan Crafts to Tibetan Imports, reflecting the many cultures of Portland. Open every weekend from March through Christmas.

ARTEMISIA
110 S.E. 28th Ave., Portland: 503-232-8224
collagewithnature.com
It's all about terrariums here, with all the shells, rocks and other things you need to create a great one.

BEAM & ANCHOR
2710 N Interstate Ave, Portland, 503-367-3230
www.beamandanchor.com
Great place to shop for one-of-a-kind gifts. Here you'll find custom furniture, ceramics, jewelry, candles, knives, pillows, kitchenware, paper goods, leather, apothecary, art, and accessories. Venue includes several working art studios including a wood-working shop.

DANNER
12021 NE Airport Way, Portland, 503-251-1111
www.danner.com
Local outlet of Danner boots known for superior craftsmanship. Boots for hiking, hunting, work, military, and law enforcement. You'll also find American made clothing ideally suited for the urban lumberjack.

HAUNT
811 E. Burnside, Suite 113, Portland: 503-928-7266
http://hauntstudio.blogspot.com/
Vintage-inspired fashion and knits in this hot little shop.

HILLSDALE FARMERS' MARKET
1509 SW Sunset Blvd #2e, Portland: 503-475-6555
hillsdalefarmersmarket.com
Runs **weekly** on Sunday from May – November, then **twice monthly** December - April.

HOUSE OF VINTAGE
3315 B SE Hawthorne Blvd., 503-236-1991
www.houseofvintagenw.com/portland/
Here you'll find over 50 vendors occupying small spaces within the big store, so you get 50 different sensibilities that have collected all this vintage stuff: clothes, accessories, jewelry, handbags, furnishings, other items for the home. It's endless. A browser's dream. A claustrophobic's nightmare.

JOHN HELMER HABERDASHER
969 SW Broadway, 503-223-4976
www.johnhelmer.com
Fine men's clothing since 1921. Nothing too trendy here, but that's why you'll like it. Great place to get good hats for men, even Irish tweed caps, French berets, safari hats, you name it. In addition to great headware, they have gorgeous accessories, men's suits, shirts, outerware, smoking jackets, and they sell Alden Shoes, a factory making shoes in Massachusetts since 1884. Oh, and the socks, by God, to go with them! Come here for that seersucker suit you've been meaning to buy but kept putting it off.

MAGPIE
1960 SE Hawthorne Blvd, Portland, 503-946-1153
Wildly varied collection of everything from sunglasses to tops, dresses, suits, men's and women's clothing, hats, handbags, lots of costume jewelry.

MACHUS
Central Eastside, 542 E Burnside, 503-206-8626
www.machusonline.com
While you're going to see your fair share of consignment shops and vintage clothing boutiques on Burnside in the Central Eastside, there's this bright beacon for the latest fashions: Cast of Vices, Billy Kirk, Field Scout, Lauren Main, Alexander Wang, Red Wing and many, many others in this dizzying collection. Big emphasis on high quality denim, but lots of accessories, funky jewelry, outerware, tops and pants.

MISSISSIPPI RECORDS
5202 N. Albina Ave., Portland: 503-282-2990
https://www.facebook.com/pages/Mississippi-Records/53429836509
Vinyl heaven for those collecting the old stuff: old-time Americana, retro funk, rare blues albums.

MONOGRAPH BOOKWERKS
5005 N.E. 27th Ave., Portland: 503-284-5005
monographbookwerks.com
A nice little find, and when I say little, I mean little. It can't be 200 square feet. But in here you'll find an art bookstore with old prints, clay pottery, little collectible pieces and other oddities. (Artists come to speak here, so find out the schedule.)

POWELL'S BOOKS
1005 W. Burnside St., 503-228-4651
www.powells.com
One of the most famous bookstores in America and rightly so. As a writer myself, I consider this place to be a shrine, and I never come to Portland without

stopping in. Aisles and aisles of new, used and out-of-print books. What the Strand is to New York, Powell's is to the whole West Coast. Bring your kids here so they can experience an honest-to-god bookstore. I think, even as the ebook craze ravishes the bookstore segment of the economy, there will always be a place for stores as carefully run as Powell's. It's a wonderful maze in which to get lost while you discover something new.

RISTRETTO ROASTERS
3808 N. Williams St., 503-288-8667
222 SW Columbia St, Portland, 503-477-9087
www.ristrettoroasters.com
They roast their coffees every day and deliver them to their 2 retail locations, dozens of wholesale clients and Whole Foods. Coffee changes frequently based on seasons and what owner Din Johnson has sourced.

SALT & STRAW
3345 SE Division St., 503-208-2054
www.saltandstraw.com
Highest quality ice cream (we like the chocolate), what they call "farm-to-cone ice cream." Try the candycap mushroom with its maple flavor, or the bourbon barrel aged stout flavor.

SCHOOLHOUSE ELECTRIC
2181 NW Nicolai St, Portland, 503-782-6118
www.schoolhouseelectric.com
Unique storefront in what was a wool warehouse at one time dating back to 1910, this place offers a selection of vintage style furniture, hand-crafted

herringbone rugs, exposed-bulb chandeliers, lighting, home goods, hardware, tufted headboards and jewelry. This is where you can find unique light fixtures.

SMART FOOD SERVICE
1825 NW 19th Ave, Portland: 503-224-0012
smartfoodservice.com
This is a restaurant supply store that's fun to browse thorough.

SOUTHEAST WINE COLECTIVE
2425 SE 35th Pl., 503-208-2061
www.sewinecollective.com
This is a place where they make wine—four wineries share the equipment here. What you come for is the tasting room they maintain up front. Get a charcuterie or cheese platter and settle down for a nice afternoon.

STAND UP COMEDY
511 SW Broadway, 503-233-3382
www.shopstandingup.us
Great boutique for avant-garde men's and women's clothing, jewelry, shoes, belts, handbags. Unusual objects for the home. Excellent place to get a gift. Discriminating selection. (They also carry small press books focusing on Portland.)

STERLING COFFEE ROASTERS
518 NW 21st Ave., Portland: 971-221-0265
sterlingcoffeeroasters.com

Stumptown is the local coffee heavyweight, but Sterling has been making news of late. Be sure to swing by here if you have a little extra time.

STEVEN SMITH TEAMAKER
110 SE Washington St, Portland, 971-254-3935
smithtea.com
Drop in here for some artisanal blends you won't find just anywhere. Very popular gathering place.

STUMPTOWN COFFEE ROASTERS
4525 SE Division St., 503-230-7702
www.stumptowncoffee.com
I've mentioned how seriously people in Portland are hooked on their coffee. This is the original location of this famous chain. (Don't overlook their excellent Cold Brew.)
Other locations in town:
Belmont – 3356 SE Belmont Street – 503-232-8889
Stark – 1026 SW Stark Street – 503-224-9060
The Annex – 100 SE Salmon Street – 503-467-4123
Downtown – 128 SW 3rd Avenue – 503-295-6144

TENDER LOVING EMPIRE
412 SW 10th Ave., Portland: 503-548-2925
tenderlovingempire.com
Curious little shop that sells things on consignment.

VINTAGE PINK
2500 SE Hawthorne Blvd., 503-224-8100
www.ilovevintagepink.com
Yet another superior vintage boutique offering fashions and accessories dating back to the 1950s.

XTABAY VINTAGE CLOTHING BOUTIQUE
2515 SE Clinton St., 503-230-2899
www.xtabayvintage.com
Appointment only. This is one of the best of Portland's numerous vintage shops. Vintage fashions (and accessories) from the 1950s, '60s and '70s. (They now have a bridal salon upstairs where they use old McCall's patterns to make some of the wedding dresses.)

WILDFANG
404 SW 10th Ave, Portland, 503-964-6746
www.wildfang.com
Funky, industrial-chic retail shop selling women's fashions for the "tom boy." Yes, women's fashions inspired by menswear. "Wildfang" means "tom boy" in German. Red Wing boots, Shades of Grey.

INDEX

A

Ace Hotel, 31
ACE HOTEL, 12
AMBONNAY CHAMPAGNE BAR, 60
American, 28, 34
American (New), 35, 45, 48
ARTEMISIA, 80
Asian Fusion, 32
AVA GENE'S, 25

B

BAMBOO, 26
BAO BAO DUMPLING HOUSE, 26
BEAM & ANCHOR, 80
Bicycles, 10
BIJOU CAFÉ, 27
BridgePort, 69
Bridgeport Village, 80

C

Cars, Avoiding, 10
CASTAGNA, 28
Central Eastside Industrial District, 8
Chinese, 26
Clackamas Town Center, 80
CLINTON STREET THEATER, 61
CLYDE COMMON, 31
Concordia Microbrewery, 19, 47
COOPERS HALL, 28
Courtyard Restaurant, 19, 47
CREMA COFFEE & BAKERY, 29
Cypress Room, 19, 47

D

DAME, 31
DANNER, 81
DAVENPORT, 32
DELUXE, 15
Departure, 21
DEPARTURE RESTAURANT, 32
Detention Bar, 19, 47
DIG A PONY, 33
Downtown PP, 80

E

EAST ENDER, 34
EASTBURN, 63
EURO TRASH, 35

F

FIRESIDE, 35
French, 45, 46
FRIED EGG I'M IN LOVE, 36
From the Airport, 9
FRYING SCOTSMAN, 37
FULLER'S, 38
FULTON HOUSE BED & BREAKFAST, 13

G

GIGANTIC BREWING COMPANY, 69
GOVERNOR HOTEL, 23
GRAVY, 39
GROUND KONTROL CLASSIC ARCADE, 69

H

H&M, 80
H5O Bistro & Bar, 15
HA & VL, 40
Hair of the Dog, 69
HAN OAK, 40
HAUNT, 81
Hawthorne Avenue, 80
HEADWATERS, 40
HEATHMAN, 14
HILLSDALE FARMERS' MARKET, 81
HOLLYWOOD THEATRE, 63
Honor's Bar, 19, 47
Hopworks Urban Brewery, 69
HOSTELLING INTERNATIONAL PORTLAND-NORTHWEST, 14
HOUSE OF VINTAGE, 81
HOYT ARBORETUM, 70
HUBER'S CAFÉ, 41

I

IMPERIAL, 42
In a Car, 10
Inner Southeast, 8
INTERNATIONAL ROSE TEST GARDENS, 70
Italian, 56

J

Jake's Grill, 23

K

KACHKA, 43
KENNEDY SCHOOL, 18
Korean, 32
Kvinneakt, 73

L

LARDO, 44
LAURELHURST MARKET, 44
LAURETTA JEAN'S, 45
LE PIGEON, 45
Lloyd Center, 80
Lloyd District, 80

LOW BROW LOUNGE, 64

M

MACHUS, 83
Macy's, 80
MAGPIE, 82
MARRIOTT PORTLAND CITY CENTER, 20
MAURICE LUNCHONETTE, 46
MAX, 10
McCALL WATERFRRONT PARK, 70
McCall, Tom, 71
McMenamin, 19, 47
McMenamin brothers, 69
McMENAMINS KENNEDY SCHOOL, 47
MCMENAMINS WHITE EAGLE, 20
MEE-SEN THAI EATERY, 51
MISSISSIPPI RECORDS, 83
MONACO, 16
MONOGRAPH BOOKWERKS, 84
MULTNOMAH WHISKEY LIBRARY, 47

N

NED LUDD, 48
NINES, 21
Nines Hotel, 32
Nob Hill, 80
NORANEKO, 48
Nordstrom, 80
Northwest Film Center, 76

O

OAKS AMUSEMENT PARK CAROUSEL, 71
OLYMPIA PROVISIONS, 49
OMSI, 72
OREGON HISTORICAL SOCIETY, 72
OREGON MUSEUM OF SCIENCE AND INDUSTRY, 72
OREGON ZOO, 73
OX, 50

P

Paley, Chef Vitaly, 53
PALEY'S PLACE, 52
Pastries, 46
Pazzo, 17
PazzoBar, 17
Pearl District, 8
PINE STATE BISCUITS, 53
PIONEER COURTHOUSE SQUARE, 73
Pioneer Place, 80
PITTOCK MANSION, 74
Pizza, 56
POK POK, 53
PORTLAND AERIAL TRAM, 75
PORTLAND ART MUSEUM, 76
PORTLAND BOTTLE SHOP, 54
PORTLAND CHILDREN'S MUSEUM, 76
PORTLAND JAPANESE GARDEN, 76
Portland Saturday Market, 80
Portland Streetcar, 8
Portland Visitor Information & Services Center, 8
PORTLANDIA, 77

POWELL'S BOOKS, 84
<u>Public Transit</u>, 10

R

Red Star Tavern & Roast House, 16
REEL M INN, 65
RENATA, 55
RINGSIDE, 55
RISTRETTO ROASTERS, 85
RIVERPLACE, 21
ROGUE ALES, 77
Russian, 43

S

SALT & STRAW, 85
Sandwiches, 53
SAPPORO BELL, 78
SCHOOLHOUSE ELECTRIC, 85
SLAB, 56
Small Plates, 47
SMART FOOD SERVICE, 86
SOCIETY HOTEL, 22
SOUTHEAST WINE COLECTIVE, 86
Southern, 53
STAND UP COMEDY, 86
Steakhouse, 44
STERLING COFFEE ROASTERS, 86
STEVEN SMITH TEAMAKERS, 87
Streetcar, 10
STUMPTOWN COFFEE ROASTERS, 87

T

TASTY n SONS, 56
TENDER LOVING EMPIRE, 87
TEOTE AREPERIA, 57
TORO BRAVO, 57
Trimet, 10
TUSK, 58

V

VALENTINE'S, 66
VINTAGE PINK, 87
VINTAGE PLAZA, 16

W

WASHINGTON PARK, 78
Washington Square, 80
WATER AVENUE COFFEE, 59
Weather Machine, 73
Westfield Vancouver, 80
White Eagle Cafe and Rock 'n' Roll Hotel, 20
WILDFANG, 88
Wine Bar, 29
WORLD FORESTRY CENTER DISCOVERY MUSEUM, 78

X

XTABAY VINTAGE CLOTHING BOUTIQUE, 88

Z

ZAGS, 17

WANT 3 FREE THRILLERS?

Why, of course you do!
If you like these writers--
Vince Flynn, Brad Thor, Tom Clancy, James Patterson, David Baldacci, John Grisham, Brad Meltzer, Daniel Silva, Don DeLillo
If you like these TV series –
House of Cards, Scandal, West Wing, The Good Wife, Madam Secretary, Designated Survivor

> You'll love the **unputdownable** series about Jack Houston St. Clair, with political intrigue, romance, and loads of action and suspense.

Besides writing travel books, I've written political thrillers for many years that have delighted hundreds of thousands of readers. I want to introduce you to my work!
Send me an email and I'll send you a link where you can download the first 3 books in my bestselling series, absolutely FREE.

Mention **this book** when you email me.
andrewdelaplaine@mac.com

www.ingramcontent.com/pod-product-compliance
Lightning Source LLC
LaVergne TN
LVHW051509070426
835507LV00022B/3008